The life cycle of a
Cat

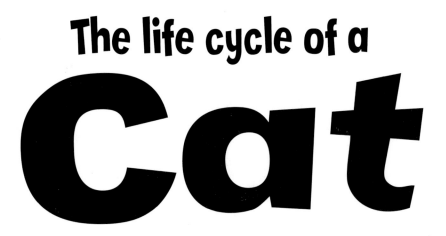

Ruth Thomson

PowerKiDS press.

New York

Published in 2008 by The Rosen Publishing Group, Inc.
29 East 21st Street, New York, NY 10010

First Edition

Photo credits: Cover main image, 4-5 Blickwinkel/ Alamy; 2 Ulrike Schanz/naturepl.com; 6, 7, cover inset center, 16, 22, 23 Aflo/naturepl.com; 8, 23 Bartussek/ARCO/naturepl.com; 9, 10, 12, 13, 14, 15, 17, 18, 23 Jane Burton/naturepl.com; cover inset top, cover inset bottom and 11, 19, 23 Wegner/ARCO/naturepl.com; 20 and 21
Bengt Lundberg/naturepl.com

Library of Congress Cataloging-in-Publication Data

Thomson, Ruth, 1949-
  Cat / Ruth Thomson. -- 1st ed.
      p. cm. -- (Learning about life cycles:
  The life cycle of a cat)
  Includes index.
  ISBN-13: 978-1-4042-3710-0 (library binding)
  ISBN-10: 1-4042-3710-0 (library binding)
  1. Cats--Life cycles--Juvenile literature. I. Title.
  SF445.7.T46 2007
  636.8--dc22
                                2006033085

Manufactured in China

Contents

Cats live here

Most cats live with people in their homes. People feed and look after cats, and give them a warm place to sleep.

What is a cat?

Pet cats belong to the animal family, which includes wild cats such as lions. All cats are meat eaters. They can run fast or **stalk** silently on their soft **paws**.

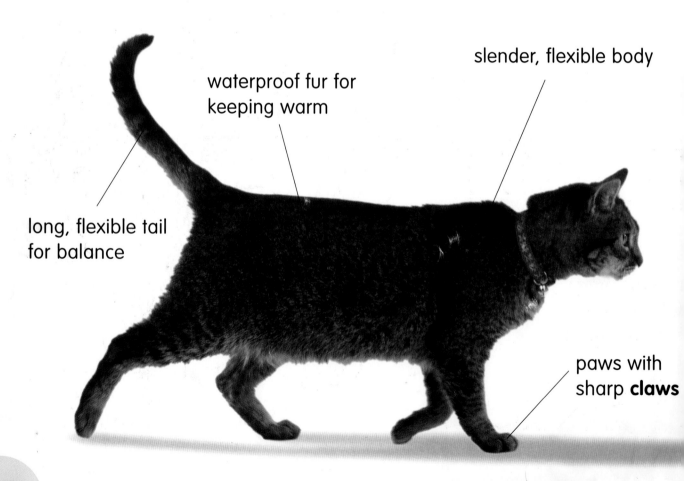

slender, flexible body

waterproof fur for keeping warm

long, flexible tail for balance

paws with sharp **claws**

Cats have very sharp senses.

large ears that can turn to pick up sounds

eyes that see well in dim light

moist nose for smelling

rough tongue for drinking and **grooming**

large, pointed side teeth for catching **prey**

whiskers for feeling things in the dark

Birth

A mother cat gives birth to a **litter** of four or five kittens. The newborn kittens are tiny and damp. Their mother licks them dry.

A newborn kitten is weak
and helpless. It cannot see
or hear, and it has no teeth.

Its legs are floppy and its **claws**
stick out from its **paws**.

Baby kittens

The kittens snuggle up to their mother to keep warm. They **suckle** on her milk. Each kitten chooses a **teat** and always suckles on the same one.

1
day

1
week

The mother begins to leave
her kittens for a short while. The kittens
sleep in a heap. They keep each other
warm when their mother is away.

10 days

Walking

After a week or so, a kitten's eyes and ears open. But it takes a few more days before the kitten can see or hear well. It can crawl around, but wails if it cannot find its mother.

Soon the kitten is strong
enough to stand and take
its first steps.

3
weeks

Growing up

The kittens begin to grow teeth. Then they can start eating kitten food and drinking water.

4 weeks

6
weeks

The kittens become very curious.
They sniff everything.
They tap objects.
They have play-fights.

7
weeks

Learning

The kitten learns from its mother how to **groom** itself. It licks its front **paw** and wipes it across its face and ears. It twists its head to groom the side of its body.

16

The mother cat helps her kittens learn hunting skills. She waves her tail as if it were moving **prey**. The kittens **stalk** and pounce on it.

8 weeks

Playing

The kittens become bolder
and stronger. They love playing.
They watch a toy on a string,
and leap into the air
to grab it.

9 weeks

The kittens
like to climb
everywhere.
They use
their **claws**
to grip.

Going outside

As the kittens grow older, they like spending time outside. They climb trees, find sunny spots to sleep, and may chase mice or birds.

10 weeks

By six months, the kittens are young cats. They like to wander as they please. They can always find their own way home.

6 months

1 year

Adult cat

Cats are fully grown when they are a year old. Now they can produce kittens of their own.

Cat life cycle

Birth
The mother cat
gives birth to four
or five kittens.

1 week
The kittens spend
all day suckling
or sleeping.

1 year
Cats are fully grown and can
have kittens of their own.

2-3 months
The kittens play, explore, and
learn to hunt inside and outside.

Glossary

claw a long curved, pointed nail at the end of an animal's **paw**

groom to clean by licking or pulling through fur

litter a family of baby animals born at the same time

paw an animal's foot

prey the animals that are killed by other animals for food

stalk to hunt an animal quietly

suckle to feed on milk from a mother

teat the part of a female animal that its babies suck to get milk

whiskers the long, stiff hairs on the face of a cat

Web Sites

Due to the changing nature of Internet links, PowerKid Press has developed an online list of Web sites related to the subject of this book. This site is regularly updated. Please use this link to access this list: www.powerkidslinks.com/llc/cat/

Index